When I'm Feeli Lonely

Written and illustrated by Trace Moroney

The Five Mile Press

When I'm feeling lonely
I feel like I am all by myself in the world
. . . and nobody loves me.

When I'm feeling lonely
it seems like everyone is having fun
– except me.

Feeling lonely can make you think

there is no one else like you.

Some things that make me
feel lonely are . . .
when I look or feel different
from other people . . .

or when I need help
and everyone just seems
too busy . . .

or when I find it hard to talk about
how I feel – even if there are lots
of people around.

Everyone has moments when they feel lonely,
or different, or that they don't fit in.

When I'm feeling lonely
I try to remember that there are

hundreds and thousands

of people around the world
who feel the same way . . .

or I call my best friend Scarlett who reminds me of all the things we like to do that are the same.

Feeling lonely doesn't have to be scary.
It can give me time to listen to my own feelings,
and work things out by myself . . .

and that makes me feel really good!

Sometimes, the things that make me feel "**diffeRent**" are the same things that my friends and family really like about me!